300

SCIENCE FACTS FOR KIDS

KENTISH PRESS

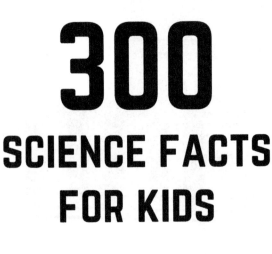

300
SCIENCE FACTS
FOR KIDS

KENTISH PRESS ARE AN INDEPENDENT SELF-PUBLISHING TEAM COMMITTED TO PRODUCING THE BEST QUALITY BOOKS POSSIBLE.

ALL INFORMATION IN THIS BOOK IS CORRECT AT THE TIME OF PUBLICATION (MAY 2022), BUT IF YOU NOTICE ANYTHING THAT DOESN'T SEEM RIGHT AT THE TIME OF USING THE BOOK THEN PLEASE LET US KNOW AT KENTISHPRESS@GMAIL.COM AND WE WILL BE HAPPY TO HELP.

IF YOU ENJOYED THIS BOOK, WE ALSO HAVE A NUMBER OF OTHER FACT BOOKS ON AMAZON COVERING A RANGE OF DIFFERENT TOPICS.

KENTISH PRESS

The air at the summit of Mount Everest, 29,029 feet up, is only a third as thick as the air at sea level.

The tallest tree ever recorded was an Australian Eucalyptus in 1872, which was measured at a height of 435 feet tall.

Christian Barnard performed the first heart transplant in 1967. After the surgery the patient lived for 18 days.

The Ebola virus kills 4 out of 5 people that it infects.

The Wright brothers were responsible for the first flight of an aircraft. But the wingspan of a modern Boeing 747 is in fact bigger than the distance the Wright brothers first flew.

In 1962 a massive advancement was made in wireless communication when the first satellite that was capable of relaying telephone and satellite signals was launched.

In another 5 billion years the sun will run out of energy and will turn into a red giant.

Giraffes never lie down, and they often only sleep for 20 minutes in a day!

If your stomach did not have the mucus lining, it would begin to digest itself.

On the day that Alexander Graham Bell was buried, the entire US telephone system was shut down for 1 minute in tribute.

The low frequency call of the humpback whale is the loudest noise made by a living creature. It is louder than the Concorde and can be heard up to 500 miles away.

The largest eyes on the planet, measuring 15 inches, belong to the giant squid.

The Universe contains over 100 billion galaxies, and the largest of these galaxies has a million, million stars.

When a wound is infested with maggots, it heals faster and is less likely to get infected or have gangrene.

The longest glacier in Antarctica, the Lambert Glacier, is 250 miles long and 40 miles wide.

Honey bees can fly at speeds of up to 15 miles per hour.

A healthy person has 6,000 million, million, million haemoglobin molecules.

Inuit people are known for rarely having heart attacks - this is due to their salmon rich and low cholesterol diet.

Inbreeding causes 3 out of every 10 Dalmatian dogs to suffer from a hearing disability.

The world's smallest winged insect, the Tanzanian parasitic wasp, is smaller than the eye of a housefly.

If the Sun were the size of a beach ball, then Jupiter would be the size of a golf ball and the Earth would be as small as a pea.

It would take over an hour for a heavy object to sink 6.7 miles down to the deepest part of the ocean.

There are more living organisms on the skin of each human than there are humans on the face of the Earth.

The grey whale migrates 12,500 miles, from the Arctic to Mexico and back, every year.

Koalas sleep an average of 22 hours a day, two hours more than the sloth.

It is possible for a baby to be born with a tooth - the odds are about 1 in 2,000.

With every single second that passes, the Universe expands by a billion miles in every direction.

If you were to travel at the speed of light and head to Andromeda, the closest large galaxy, it would take you 2 million years.

In the summer, the Eiffel tower can be 15 cm taller - this is due to the metal framework expanding in the heat.

20% of the Earth's oxygen is produced by the Amazon rainforest.

Some metals, including potassium and sodium, are so reactive that they explode when they come into contact with water.

Due to the movement of the tectonic plates, Hawaii moves 7 cm closer to Alaska every year.

Chalk is made from trillions of microscopic plankton fossils.

In 2.3 billion years, it will be too hot for life to exist on Earth. This is because the sun will continue to burn brighter and brighter over time.

Sound waves generate heat as they travel and are absorbed by materials.

According to Einstein's theory of relativity, time goes by faster at the top of a building compared to the bottom.

You cannot sink when you are in the Dead Sea, because of the high salt content of the water.

A typical smartphone would not detect touches from fingernails, rubber or certain fabrics because they lack the ions needed for the interaction.

Sandcastles can stand on their own because of the water tension between sand and water molecules.

Irrational numbers are numbers that cannot be expressed as fractions. An example of this is Pi.

There is a basilisk lizard called the Jesus Christ lizard, because of its ability to walk on water.

Every time that you see a vibration, you are in fact seeing sound.

The most abundant atoms in the Universe are hydrogen atoms, which account for about 74% of all atoms.

Rabbits and parrots can see behind themselves without moving their heads!

Elephants are the largest animals that cannot jump.

Approximately 3% of the ice in the Antarctic glacier is made up of penguin urine.

Most of the dust that you see in your house is in fact dead skin.

A battery has chemical energy in it, and it is a chemical reaction that converts chemical energy into electricity.

Milk contains calcium, which is proven to help with the strength of bones.

The Earth's inner core is 6,000 degrees Celsius, and its outer core is a mere 3,800 degrees Celsius.

Apollo 14 astronaut, Alan Shepard, played golf on the moon in 1971!

Scientists believe the Hercules beetle can lift up to 850 times its own weight.

The Great Lakes in America hold more than 20% of the world's surface freshwater.

Humans breathe in oxygen and breathe out carbon dioxide. Plants take in carbon dioxide and convert it to oxygen.

In her lifetime, a female sunfish can lay as many as 300 million eggs.

Most scientists agree that dogs and humans have been hunting partners and companions for more than 14,000 years.

6 million hours is the equivalent of 2.76 years on Pluto.

The large flying fox is the largest bat on Earth and has a wingspan of up to 5 feet.

About 70% of the Earth's surface is covered in water.

The Earth has been around for about 4 - 5 billion years, and the fascinating thing is that humans have only been around for between 0.1 - 0.2% of the time that Earth has existed!

Earth is the third planet from the Sun and is the fifth largest planet in our solar system, after Jupiter, Saturn, Uranus and Neptune.

Earth's largest and only natural satellite is the moon!

Earth is the only planet in our solar system known to support life.

The Great Barrier Reef in Australia is known to be the largest living structure on Earth. It spans about 2,000 kilometres and is composed of coral islands and reefs.

Once you eat your food, it takes your body around 12 hours to fully digest it.

Your brain contains around 100 billion nerve cells!

Your heart beats around 100,000 times a day.

The smallest bone in the human body is present in the middle part of the ear. It's called the stirrup and is only 2.8 mm long.

Your mouth produces about 1 litre of saliva per day!

Human teeth are just as strong as shark teeth!

A fully grown adult has 206 bones in their body, whereas a newborn baby has 300 bones. Some of these bones fuse together as the baby grows.

If spread out, the total surface area of adult lungs can be up to 75 square metres. This is the size of half a tennis court!

If all the blood vessels in an adult's body are laid out end to end, they will cover and circle the Earth's equator 4 times!

If all the DNA in the human body was uncoiled and put together, it would be about twice the diameter of our whole solar system.

You wouldn't be able to taste food if it weren't for saliva, because our taste buds can only detect the taste of food once it's dissolved in a liquid!

Did you know that a polar bear's fur is actually transparent, but because of the way the strands reflect light, they appear to be white.

Another cool science fact about polar bears is that their skin under the fur is actually black in colour, so it can absorb and retain heat from the sun!

The dog is known as "man's best friend" for a reason. Dogs are great helpers and can be trained to help people with disabilities, as well as performing tasks such as hunting, farming and acting as security!

Dogs have an amazing sense of hearing and can hear sounds at 4 times the distance that humans can.

Dolphins are some of the most playful sea creatures and are highly intelligent! Their brain development is similar to that of humans.

Dolphins have also been observed to live together in large groups and hunt, as well as play, together!

Elephants are the world's largest mammals that live on land.

An adult elephant needs to drink more than 200 litres of water each day!

A lion's roar can be heard from a whopping 8 kilometres away!

Lions have been observed to rest for a large part of the day, usually around 20 hours.

The blue whale, the largest animal in the world, needs to come to the surface of the water to breathe!

Octopi have three hearts, nine brains and have blue blood!

An eagle's eyes are about 4 times sharper than those of a human.

The bee hummingbird is the smallest bird in the world and the ostrich is the largest bird in the world!

The hummingbird flaps its wings extremely fast, making between 80 to 200 flaps per second to be able to hover.

The ostrich is also the fastest running bird in the world, having a running speed of 70 km per hour!

Hummingbirds are the only birds that can fly backwards.

An owl can rotate its head up to 270 degrees without moving its body! Humans can only rotate their heads about 80 degrees.

The Sun is more than 109 times larger than the size of the Earth.

Space is completely silent as there's no atmosphere for sound to travel through!

It isn't possible to walk on planets like Jupiter, Neptune, Saturn or Uranus as they don't have a solid surface! They're mostly made up of different gases.

The largest internal organ is the small intestine, despite it being called the smaller of the two intestines.

The moon doesn't emit any light of its own. The light from the sun's rays bounces off the moon and reaches the Earth in a matter of 1.25 seconds. This is how we get moonlight.

The pressure created by your heart is enough to send your blood squirting 30 feet.

The fastest growing nail is on the middle finger, and the nail on the middle finger of your dominant hand will grow the fastest of all.

No life form could survive if it were to enter a black hole, like the one at the centre of our galaxy, the Milky Way. Even light can't survive in a black hole.

The reason the ocean has waves and tides that switch from high to low is that the gravitational pulls from the moon and the sun keep changing.

Mount Everest is the highest mountain on Earth, but the highest mountain known to man is actually present on an asteroid called Vesta and is 22 km in height.

There are more stars in the universe than there are grains of sand on Earth.

In 1969, Neil Armstrong became the first man to walk on the moon.

It takes the light from the sun about 8 minutes to reach Earth.

Sound travels at a speed of 1,225 km per hour.

Hydrogen is the first element on the periodic table. It has an atomic number of 1.

Your fingernails grow faster when you are cold.

Your brain uses 10 watts of energy to think and does not feel pain.

Today, the fabrics and designs of swimwear glide more smoothly through water than our own human skin.

Pineapples take 2 years to grow.

The strawberry is the only fruit whose seeds grow on the outside.

A lightning strike can reach up to 30,000 degrees Celsius. This is around 6 times hotter than the surface of the sun.

Around 30% of the energy used in buildings is used unnecessarily.

The combustion of fossil fuels is the cause of over 86% of the energy used in the US.

The speed of light is a staggering 299,792 km per second! This is when it is travelling through a vacuum with no obstruction from the atmosphere.

Black is the most common natural hair color for humans. Red is the rarest!

Heat from the sun is captured and used to power many things on the planet. This is called solar energy. It is one of a few environmentally-friendly energy sources.

A scientist who studies biology is known as a "biologist".

The animal with the fastest punch on earth is the tiny mantis shrimp! It can punch at speeds of up to 50mph.

Cucumbers are actually a fruit and not a vegetable. They are part of the melon family.

There are around 630 different kinds of carnivorous plants. There are types that can survive in the water and others that grow from the soil.

Touching poison ivy causes an allergic reaction on the skin, as it produces a skin irritant called "urushiol".

Saturn is the planet in our solar system with the most moons - it has 82.

It takes light travelling from the sun up to 8 hours to reach Neptune.

A scientist who studies chemistry is known as a "chemist".

The bark of the willow tree was the first source of aspirin, the well-known medication used to reduce pain and fever.

Eyebrows play two important roles: they protect against rain, sweat and dirt, whilst also helping us to express our emotions.

Elephants can stay pregnant for up to 22 months.

Upwards of 75% of bottlenose dolphins are considered to be right-handed.

Light travels in straight lines, it is only when it hits an object in its way that it refracts or bends.

Electric eels can send out electric shocks of around 500 volts.

When driving at 50mph, cars use around half of their fuel just to overcome wind resistance!

There are some sharks that emit a green light, making them glow in the dark.

A scientist who studies physics is known as a "physicist".

Uranus is the only planet in our solar system that rolls on its side, like a barrel.

You can see all of the planets except Neptune and Uranus with the naked eye on a clear night, and all 8 planets can be seen with a small telescope or binoculars.

The cheetah is the fastest animal on the planet, clocking in at speeds of around 70mph.

Albert Einstein won the 1921 Nobel prize in physics.

Biology is the science of life and living things.

The human body is estimated to have 60,000 miles of blood vessels.

A cockroach can live for up to one week without its head.

The largest organ in the human body is the skin.

DNA contains the information that makes living organisms work.

Not all bacteria is bad for us - some are actually very helpful in keeping us healthy.

A neutron star spins 600 times a second.

Most viruses are so small that you have to look at them under a microscope.

Your heart is roughly the size of your fist. It also weighs about 1 pound.

The average human heart beats 100,000 times a day.

If you were to travel around the earth at the speed of light you would get around the planet 7 and a half times in a second.

An angler fish uses a small bulb-like feature to emit light to hypnotise prey before it pounces.

From space, you can clearly see the divide between east and west Germany - this is because they both use different types of lightbulb.

The human eye cannot see ultraviolet light, because there is a filter on your eye that blocks it out.

Before the blood within your veins mixes with oxygen, it is a blue colour. After it mixes with oxygen, it is then red in colour.

The human heart has many valves which are there to stop the blood flowing the wrong way.

The skeleton that is inside the body of a creature is called the "endoskeleton" and the one which is outside the body is known as the "exoskeleton".

The study of the human skeleton is known as "orthopaedics".

The biggest joint in the human body is the knee!

In order for a rocket to escape the Earth's gravity, it must travel at a speed of at least 7 miles a second.

If every star in the Milky Way was a grain of salt they would fill an Olympic sized swimming pool.

The arm is one of the most commonly broken bones in the human body.

There have been less than 600 people that have flown to space.

There are only two elements that are liquid at room temperature - bromine and mercury.

Copper and gold are the only two non-silvery metals.

Micro-organisms have been brought back to life after being frozen in perma-frost for 3 million years.

Water is unlike other objects when it freezes, as water expands in its solid state.

There is a volcano located on mars that is more than twice the size of Mt Everest.

There are roughly 250 grams of salt in the human body.

Plants turn light from the sun into food. This process is called "photosynthesis".

An octopus weighing up to 600 pounds can squeeze into a hole the size of a quarter.

In the Universe, the most abundant element is hydrogen, although nitrogen is the most abundant in the Earth's atmosphere.

Your funny bone isn't in fact a bone, it is actually a nerve.

The largest dinosaur ever discovered was Seismosaurus who was over 100 feet long and weighed up to 80 tonnes.

In 2012, Felix Baumgartner decided he was going to skydive from the edge of space, falling from a height of 38,969.4 metres.

In the 14th century, the black plague killed 75,000,000 people. The disease was carried by fleas that were hosted by the black rat.

A typical hurricane produces the energy equivalent to 8,000 one-megaton bombs.

Flamingos can only eat when their heads are upside down.

Sound travels at speeds up to 4.3 times faster in water than in air.

The loudest sound ever to be heard on earth was the eruption of Krakatoa in 1883. The eruption also caused tsunami waves as high as 46 metres.

Much like water, liquid air has a bluish tint.

Copper is the only metal that is naturally antibacterial.

Ununoctium is the heaviest element found so far, with atomic number 118.

Under normal conditions, oil and water will not mix.

Dry ice is the solid state of carbon dioxide.

The footprints that have been left on the moon will never go - this is because there is no wind on the moon.

The brain operates on the same amount of power as a 10-watt light bulb.

The brain only makes up about 2% of our body mass, yet consumes more oxygen than any other organ in the body, using up 20% of the oxygen that enters the bloodstream.

Facial hair grows faster than any other hair on the body.

Mercury and Venus are the only planets in our solar system to not have any moons.

One of Saturn's moons, Enceladus, reflects 90% of the sun's light.

The most expensive substance in the world is the element californium.

The stable element with the highest density is osmium.

Edmund Halley is an English astronomer, who discovered that the comets orbit the sun - he even has one named after him!

Glass is actually a liquid, which flows extremely slowly.

Diamond and graphite are both made up of only carbon.

Mars is red because of the amount of iron oxide that it contains.

During the day, the moon reaches temperatures of around 224 degrees Fahrenheit, but at night will get as cold as -243 degrees Fahrenheit.

Venus is the only planet that spins clockwise.

One single teaspoon of a neutron star would weigh a staggering six billion tons.

The dinosaurs lived in a prehistoric age called the Mesozoic Era

A day on the planet Neptune is shorter than a day on Earth, at only 16 hours long.

It takes 8 minutes and 19 seconds for light to travel from the sun to Earth.

You can't hear sounds in space. This is because space is a vacuum.

The surface of the sun and the Earth's core are the same temperature.

Saturn's rings are made up of trillions of pieces of floating ice that orbit the planet.

A quarter of your bones are in your feet.

Most people know that every human has a unique fingerprint, but we also have unique tongue prints too!

Your blood has a similar salt content to the oceans.

A dog's sense of smell is around 100,000 times as strong as a human's, however they have one sixth the number of taste buds.

Your ears and nose never stop growing.

50% of the world's oxygen is produced by the sea.

The acid in the human stomach can dissolve razor blades.

NASA estimates that in the Milky Way there are 400 billion stars. And it is estimated that there are 3 trillion trees on Earth, which means that there are more trees on Planet Earth than stars in the Milky Way.

You see things upside down - your brain then has to flip them the right way up.

Light is made up of all the colours mixed together. White light can be split up to reveal red, orange, yellow, green, blue, indigo and violet.

A photon can travel from the sun to Earth in just over 8 minutes, but it takes the same photon 40,000 years to travel from the core of the sun to the sun's surface.

The hottest temperature ever recorded on earth was recorded in Furnace Creek, California. The staggering heat reached as high as 56 degrees Celsius.

The deepest part of any ocean in the world is the Mariana Trench in the Pacific, with a depth of 35,797 feet.

Light is measured in wavelengths on the electromagnetic spectrum. This spectrum includes all the different types of light and other types of waves too.

Animals that only come out at night are known as nocturnal. They are creatures such as bats, badgers and foxes.

Thomas Edison, an American scientist, was responsible for the invention of the lightbulb.

The northern lights are a display of coloured lights that appear over the North Pole. They occur when the light from the sun reacts with the gases in the Earth's atmosphere.

Plastic takes an average of 450 years to decompose.

It is in fact the male seahorse who gives birth, not the female.

The craters on the planet Mercury are named after famous musicians, artists and authors.

Humans do actually emit a bioluminescent light, although it is too weak to be seen by the human eye.

The human brain isn't fully developed until you reach the age of 25. It contains around 60% fat.

When a neutron on the brain is stimulated, the signal travels at an impressive 268 mph.

Women's hearts beat faster than men's. The main reason for this is simply that, on average, women tend to be smaller than men and have less mass to pump blood to.

Your left lung is slightly smaller than your right lung in order to allow room for the heart.

Feet have 500,000 sweat glands and can produce more than a pint of sweat a day.

Believe it or not, you do not technically see with your eyes; you do, in fact, see with your brain, with your eyes acting as a camera.

Sunlight can only reach a depth of around 80 metres. This means that at depths lower than than this it is pitch black.

There is one species of jellyfish that are immortal. They revert back to their child state after having babies.

There are so many ants that there are enough for every person on earth to have 1 million ants as pets.

Animals that have smaller bodies and faster metabolisms, such as chipmunks and squirrels, see in slow motion.

Earwax production is a very important part of your ear's defence system. It protects the delicate inner ear from bacteria, fungus, dirt and even insects. It also cleans and lubricates the ear canal.

During your lifetime, you will produce enough saliva to fill two swimming pools.

There are only roughly a third of the population that have 20-20 vision.

The human nose can remember up to 50,000 scents.

There was once a species of penguin called the colossal penguin that stood as tall as 2.03 metres, although they are sadly extinct.

Reindeers have a clever way of dealing with lower light levels in winter - their eyeballs turn a slightly blue colour.

Have you ever thought about how much a cloud weighs? The average cumulus cloud weighs a million pounds.

Bananas contain an element called potassium, and since potassium decays, that makes bananas radioactive. Although don't worry, you would need to eat 10 million bananas in one sitting to die.

Due to something called the Mpemba effect, hot water freezes faster than cold water.

A human's genome consists of as many as 145 genes that have jumped from bacteria, fungi and other single-celled organisms.

By the time that you turn 60, you are likely to have lost about half of your taste buds.

The likelihood that you snore in your sleep increases as you get older.

A 10-year study in Scotland showed that you are 20% more likely to die of a heart attack on a Monday.

The human body can go longer without food than without sleep.

The atmospheres in Neptune, Uranus and Saturn have such extreme pressure that they can crystallise carbon atoms and turn them into diamonds.

Since dinosaurs first roamed the Earth, it is believed that up to 2.5 billion T-rex set foot on the planet.

The sting of the box jellyfish triggers something known as Irukandji syndrome, which causes you to feel a growing sense of dread that can become so dramatic people have begged doctors to put them out of their misery.

Water can exist in all three states (solid, liquid and gas) at the same time - this is called the triple point.

The driest part of Planet Earth is Aswan in Egypt, where the average rainfall is 0.02 inches a year.

When helium is cooled to a temperature of -273 degrees Celsius, it turns into a super fluid. This means it can flow without friction and can scale the sides of objects against the pull of gravity.

After being sunburnt, it can take cells up to 15 months to completely recover.

A human head remains conscious for about 15 to 20 seconds after it has been decapitated.

Honey is a food that will never go bad. This is due to the high sugar levels.

Albert Einstein developed the theory of relativity.

Clouds are created when moist air rises into the sky and the water droplets cool.

Archimedes discovered the "buoyancy theory", which states that if something is placed into water then the weight of the object is equalled in the weight of the water displaced.

A typical phone camera can capture 20 or 30 megapixels, whereas the human eye could capture up to 576 megapixels.

In your lifetime, you are likely to walk roughly far enough to walk around the Earth 5 times - this is a distance of 110,000 miles.

One of the brightest stars in the sky, Betelgeuse, could explode, turning from a supergiant to a supernova. This would light our sky for up to 2 months.

A rattlesnake's fangs are actually hollow and inject the poison into their prey.

It takes an individual blood cell around about 60 seconds to complete a circuit of the body.

In the periodic table there are 118 chemical elements. Out of these, 94 occur naturally, the others being man-made.

The Earth spins at a speed of 1,000 mph and travels through space at a speed of 67,000 mph.

The temperatures in Antarctica can reach a chilling -35 degrees Celsius.

The largest ever hailstone weighed over 1kg and fell in Bangladesh in 1986.

If you could drive your car straight up you would arrive in space in just over an hour.

Humans can get invasive tapeworms that can grow to a length of 22 metres.

Dinosaurs were made extinct on Planet Earth before the Rockies and the Alps existed.

The Australian billygoat plum contains 100 times more vitamin C than an orange.

It is impossible to burp in space! This is because on Earth, gravity makes your food stay separate from the gases of the burp. But the lack of gravity in space means that you would just be sick.

Almost all mammals have two sets of teeth in their lifetime, however reptiles are different - crocodiles can grow up to 50 sets of teeth!

Nearly 85% of all plant life on Earth is found in the ocean.

Ginko Biloba is the oldest living tree species, at around 250 million years old.

Viruses such as the coronavirus cannot affect bats.

Bees sense an electric field to know whether another bee has just visited the same flower.

The sound a hummingbird makes comes from the vibrations of its wings against the air.

Crocodiles consume stones and utilise them for balance in water, as well as to grind food during digestion.

In one single bound, a kangaroo can jump 27 feet.

Hippos grow to be somewhere between 2,000 and 3,000 pounds, yet they can run at speeds of up to 30 miles per hour.

Emperor penguins can dive down to depths of 1,755 feet in order to find food.

Great white sharks can smell blood from a distance of up to 3 miles away.

Axolotls can regenerate a missing limb, tail, spinal cord, parts of their brain, heart, lower jaw and other organs.

All clownfish are born as males, and then some of them turn into females if the Alpha female dies.

20% of cockroaches can survive a high atomic bomb level of radiation.

The tissues that connect the muscles to the bones are called tendons.

Scientists believe that all of the 7 continents were once part of one big landmass on the planet, known as Pangea.

The first ever living creature to be cloned was a sheep named Dolly.

Alexander Fleming was the scientist responsible for the discovery of Penicillin.

The International Space Station is a hub for astronauts that orbits the planet at a height of 240 miles.

In 1664, Sir Isaac Newton figured out the workings of the Earth's gravity. It is widely known that an apple falling from a tree sparked his interest in this.

A candela is the unit of measurement for luminosity.

The study of animals is called zoology.

Sputnik I, the world's first satellite, was launched by the Soviet Union on October 4, 1957.

The first living thing sent into space was a fruit fly.

Laika is a very famous dog, known for being the first dog that was sent into orbit. Sadly, she is still out in space, orbiting.

New Zealand is home to the tuatara, an animal who was likely alive during the same time the dinosaurs roamed the earth

It is estimated that we have only explored 5% of the ocean.

Printed in Great Britain
by Amazon